Smokey!
The Ultimate Wood Pellet Grill Cookbook - Starters

50 Easy-to-Prepare Mouthwatering Starters Recipes to Turn You into a Smoking Professional

Phil Ward

Contents

Introduction to Wood Pellet Grilling/Smoking

Why a Wood Pellet Smoker-Grill?

 The wood pellet grill not only provides the moistest foods you have ever tasted, but it's the simplest to use and sustain. Everything is controlled by software. Make sure your hopper is full of wood pellets, and your device is attached to a power source.

The auger and fan are the only moving pieces in the wood pellet smoker-grill. Other smoker-grill styles have often had a tough time keeping stable temperatures due to the need to continually track the devices. For wood pellet smoker-grills, this is not required since they're built to keep temperatures consistent.

Most Trendy Models

Wood pellet grills merge the comfort of a barbecue grill with the taste and quality of a wood smoker, enabling you to set it and forget it. Plus, since they plug into a normal electrical socket, they do not need natural gas or propane.

From gas grills to charcoal grills, indoor grills, and beyond, it is essential to determine the right grill for you. The features of a grill such as simplicity of use and efficiency, as well as heating symmetry and cooking speed, are of utmost importance. Temperature regulation and range are critical for pellet grills. Factors such as the quality of material used, the protection it offers, the control panel, pellet dispensing mechanism, and hopper size should all be taken into account when purchasing a grill.

Considering the factors stated above, below is a list of wood pellets that are recommended. The top picks are full of features that make a perfect pellet grill, and they come from brands that are known and trusted. You will notice several sizes for any form of pellet grill and versions with unique features like functionality, Wi-Fi access, and outstanding guarantees. The safest pellet grills to purchase are as follows:

Traeger Pro Series Grill 575

D2 direct drive dynamically controls doses of pellets and airflow for optimal temperature control.

Specifications

Traeger is associated with pellet grills, and they were the first company to produce them. They're among the most common in the industry and can be used as a barbecue, smoker, or oven with precise temperature regulation. The manufactured logic sets them apart; Traeger's latest grills (including this 575 Pro) have a direct drive D2, which doses pellets and changes air flow depending on the internal setting tracked every 30 seconds by sensors.

The temperature range of the Pro 575 is 165° to 500° Fahrenheit, so it can be used for anything from barbecuing to smoking, braising, frying, and roasting. It also links to an interface with over 1,500 recipes, enabling you to program it straight from your computer and track the cooking process while doing so. You can fit as many as 16 burgers or chickens on it, plenty to feed the family and neighbors.

- Cooking surface: 572 square-inch
- Hopper capacity: 18-pound

Z Grills Wood Pellet Grill & Smoker

This Z Grills pellet grill has over 400 favorable reviews on Amazon, and this new-sounding business has been producing grills for other brands for more than 30 years. It began selling under its own label in 2017, helping it to retain its low price point. This grill has a huge cooking surface and is made of stainless steel. It has new temperature sensors that vary from 180° to 450° Fahrenheit. Although the grease collector is popular, reviewers like how simple it is to clean. It also has a complimentary grill shield.

- Cooking surface: 504 square-inch
- Hopper capacity: 20-pound

Green Mountain Davy Crockett Pellet Grill

If you are looking for a smart alternative, we suggest Green Mountain's Davy Crockett model. It has foldable legs, meaning it can take up less room in the car on game day. It is perfect for a day of tailgating or camping. It is the only compact solution with digital controls and an incorporated thermometer (called Sense-Mate) to track your beef's internal meat temperature. And, if you are too preoccupied with the game to check on your dinner, you can do it from your phone, thanks to Wi-Fi capabilities. The software also has a built-in meal timer, so you will know when it's time to feed. The cooking area is limited.

- Cooking surface: 219 square-inch
- Hopper capacity: 9-pound

Pit Boss 700FB Pellet Grill

Given its price, build quality, and capability, this is an excellent starter pellet grill. With its dial temperature monitor and quick readout show, it's a breeze to use. In addition to the multitude of grill cooking possibilities already anticipated from a pellet grill (barbecuing, grilling, and smoking), you can bake, reheat, chargrill, barbecue, and sear your food on this all-in-one device thanks to the slide-plate frame broiler. The manufacturer believes that with 700 square inches of cooking area, including the second-tier rack, you can make over 30 burgers at once.

- Cooking surface: 700 square-inch with top rack
- Hopper capacity: 21-pound

Camp Chef Woodwind Pellet Grill with Sear Box

Pellet grills have a reputation for not searing a steak as easily as a barbecue or gas grill. Camp Chef's Woodwind with Sear Box alternative can be used as a smoker, as well as a searing barbecue. For simple temperature regulation and consistent results, use the wood pellet grill, then finish with grill marks on the cast iron plate, which can hit temperatures of up to 900° Fahrenheit. Its ash-removal method makes it simpler to clean than others since ash is collected in an easy-to-remove cup beneath the smokebox. When attached, the sear box takes the role of a side rack.

- Cooking surface 429 square-inch plus 141 square-inch in the upper rack
- Hopper capacity: 24-pound

Temperature Control

The wood pellet grill just about gains the upper hand. "Place it and forget it", says Ron Popeil of his Ronco rotisserie. As we saw earlier, the controller controls the rate of pellet flow and the fan to preserve your set-point temperature. Most manufacturers either use a third-party controller or create their own. Not every controller is the same. Some are preferable to others, and this should be considered when purchasing a wood pellet grill. Look for the controller that allows for precise temperature regulation. Analog, optical, and PID controllers are the three basic categories of controllers.

The most basic unit is an analog controller that comes with only 3 options of heating. These 3 options are low, medium, and high smoke. The bulk of these controllers are located on entry-level systems. They normally do not have a temperature probe, such as an RTD or a thermocouple, to have a feedback loop. It is the least attractive remote, and I would not purchase a machine that has one. The temperature on these systems fluctuates wildly and is unable to compensate for changes in ambient temperatures. The only power you have is the auger on and off timeframes for medium, low, and heavy, which the grill maker typically fixes.

A feedback loop is provided by a digital controller using an RTD temperature probe. A 25° Fahrenheit increment setting is standard on most digital controllers. Any digital controls may be used to replace LMH controllers with the use of an RTD temperature probe. When you hit the preset temperature, the controller runs the drill for a certain number of seconds, then turns off for a certain number of seconds and goes into idle mode before the temperature deviates a preset level, just like your home's thermostat. At that point, the loop starts again. It would help if you changed the idle mode on certain digital controls to compensate for ambient temperatures.

The most modern controllers are additive, integral, derivative (PID) controllers. They equate the target temperature to the observed temperature using a control loop input from a thermocouple temperature probe and change parameters accordingly. They encourage you to adjust the temperature of your cooking in 5-degree intervals. The PID controller controls the auger feed rate, and, in certain situations, the fan variable speeds to reduce temperature fluctuations and keep the temperature within 5° Fahrenheit of the fixed temperature, resulting in highly precise temperature regulation. PID-type controllers are standard on most high-end wood pellet grills, and they use optimization algorithms fine-tuned for the units.

Various controllers, such as the digital control panel of Pellet Boss (MAK Grills), have 1 or more meat temperature probes and custom programming elements to improve your cooking experience while giving you complete control over any element of your cook.

Choose a wood pellet grill with a digital controller at the very least, and ideally one with a PID-based controller.

Smoking vs Grilling

Smoking

What it is:

Smoking is the method of using smoke and low, indirect heat to cook and preserve foods, particularly meat. It has been used to prevent food from spoiling since the time of the savages.

Refrigerators are now used less for storage and more for imparting smoky taste and tenderness to poultry, foods, and fish by cooking them at low temperatures for prolonged periods.

It is all focused on science. Flaming breaks down the collagen in meat, resulting in tenderness that melts in your mouth. To get the best performance, season the meat with a dry rub or brine before smoking it.

Equipment:

Metal chambers heated with steam, charcoal, or wood chips generate low and steady heat (between 200° and 250° Fahrenheit) and a tone of smoke in advanced meat smokers. If you go for wood, each form of wood has a distinct taste, and there are many to choose from. Though gas and charcoal grills may be adapted to smoke meats, smokers designed exclusively for smoking are the simplest for beginners to use.

Characteristics:

A smoke ring, a pink-tinged coating of meat just under the meat's crust or "bark," can be seen on nearly all smoked meats. It happens because nitrogen dioxide in smoke stops myoglobin from browning the beef. It is a hallmark of steady-smoked beef, but many scientists say it could be manipulated with sodium nitrite or curing salt (pink).

Recipes to try:

For your next Thanksgiving meal, consider traditional smoked ribs and brisket, or branch out to smoked chicken and trout.

Grilling

What it is:

Grilling meat means exposing it to high glowing heat, usually done on grates set over a heat source like charcoal or wood.

Making a caramelized crust on the exterior of the grilled beef helps to seal in moisture and cook the inside. Fun fact: backyard grilling as we know it originated after World War II, as the middle class migrated to the suburbs.

Equipment:

Grills are available in various forms, shapes, sizes, and heat sources, ranging from charcoal to petrol. Charcoal grills provide a smokier taste, which is perfect for flavorful steaks and burgers. Gas grills fueled by propane are more popular and can cook anything from veggies to hot dogs.

"An immediate read thermometer is your best option for ensuring the meat and fish are grilled to the correct temperature," says grill master Bobby Flay of other equipment. Tongs are often good for transferring food from the grill to the plate, and there are several fancy devices to use if you are feeling adventurous.

Characteristics:

Since it uses direct heat to cook the meats or other ingredients, grilling is a far quicker option than smoking. It leaves a crusty, blackened char on the outside of the beef, which tests suggest may be harmful if consumed in large quantities. A grill is more flexible than smoking in that it can cook pizza, veggies, and even fruit.

Recipes to try:

At your next cookout, consider pizza, burgers, or salmon, and for the vegetarians, try any of those meat-free recipes that cook well on a barbecue.

Grilling vs Smoking: Which One to Choose?

The most significant difference between smoking and grilling is the amount of time needed. Smoking will take all day and needs regular temperature control to ensure that the meat cooks uniformly. While grilling is more convenient and faster, smoking produces a tender and tasty product that is almost impossible to duplicate.

Slighter meats like chicken and steak cook best on a grill, whereas larger meats like ribs and briskets profit from big smokers. You will serve tasty food to friends and relatives at this summer's barbecues, regardless of the tool you choose. Grilling is about rapidly cooking food over a high heat source (fueled by gas or charcoal). In the case of grilling, hot and quick means cooking at 350° Fahrenheit or higher in less than one hour. While smoking is just like a more intense form of barbecuing: you are cooking the meat with smoke through roiling chunks or pieces of hickory, apple, mesquite, or cherry, which imparts its own taste to the meat.

Smoking takes place at a lower temperature than grilling to ensure that the smoky taste pervades the meat while still cooking it thoroughly. To smoke food, your grill should be set around 125° to 175° Fahrenheit; any hotter, and the exterior sections of the food will cook very quickly, creating a barrier that the smoke cannot pass through. But the grilling temperatures should be about 450° to 500° Fahrenheit for things like chops and steaks to enable for quick cooking times. Remember that the tenderest pieces, such as strip steaks, ribeye steaks, rib and small loin primal pieces and T-bones are the best for grilling. A great way to maintain the tenderness and avoid drying out and overcooking is to cook them quickly. Cooking a juicy, tasty slice of meat over a hot flame for a brief period is the perfect way to do it.

1. Spicy & Smoked Cashews

Preparation time: 5 mins

Cooking time: 1 hour

Servings: 6

Ingredients

- One tbsp chili paste
- One tbsp simple syrup
- Zest of one lemon
- A half tbsp chopped rosemary
- One tsp hot pepper flakes
- One pinch cayenne powder
- One lb cashews

Instructions

1. Set grill temperature to 220° F, then keep the lid closed for fifteen mins.
2. Combine the syrup, chili paste, rosemary, lemon zest, cayenne & red pepper flakes in a small bowl. Pour the mixture over the cashews and thoroughly mix to coat.
3. On a sheet tray spread the cashews. Put them straight on the grill grate. Cook the nuts for around one hour, stirring sometimes.
4. Take the cashews from the grill, allow to cool & serve.

2. Asian Jumbo Shrimps

Preparation time: 2 hours

Cooking time: 5 mins

Servings: 4

Ingredients

- Four lbs jumbo shrimps
- One cup soy sauce
- One cup teriyaki sauce
- One cup white vermouth
- One cup olive oil
- One clove garlic, chopped
- One tsp fresh ginger, grated
- One tsp chicken rub

Instructions

1. Cut the shrimp heads, shell them and remove the & black veins.
2. In a small bowl combine all the other ingredients; add the shrimps & mix thoroughly. Put the shrimp in the refrigerator & let marinate for 2-4 hours.
3. Set grill temperature to 450°F, then keep the lid closed for fifteen mins.
4. Drain the shrimp from the marinade & thread them onto pre-soaked wooden skewers.
5. Put the shrimp skewers on the grill grate, close the lid, & cook for around three mins.
6. Flip the shrimp skewers, close the lid & cook for an extra three mins.
7. Take the skewers from the grill & serve.

3. Exotic Shrimp Jalapeños

Preparation time: 10 mins

Cooking time: 55 mins

Servings: 6

Ingredients

- Eight shrimp shelled & deveined
- Half tsp chicken rub
- One tbsp olive oil
- Six jalapeño peppers
- Eight oz cream cheese
- Two tbsp chopped coriander
- Half cup dry coconut flakes
- Twelve slices smoked bacon

Instructions

1. Set grill temperature to 420°F, then keep the lid closed for fifteen mins.
2. Season the shrimps with the olive oil & chicken rub.
3. Put the shrimps on the grill grate & cook them for around five mins each side.
4. Remove the shrimp & allow to cool.
5. Lower the temp of the grill to 320°F.
6. Cut the peppers in half & remove the seeds.
7. In a blender, mince the shrimp together with the softened cream cheese, & coriander.
8. Fill each pepper half with the mixture and sprinkle coconut flakes on top.
9. Wrap every stuffed half pepper with a bacon slice & put them on a baking sheet, lined with foil.
10. Cook the peppers for around 45 mins or until the bacon gets golden & crispy. Serve.

4. Grilled Garlic Bread

• Half cup parmesan cheese, grated

Preparation time: 10 mins

Cooking time: 20 mins

Servings: 4

Ingredients

• One baguette or bread loaf
• Half cup butter, softened
• Half cup mayonnaise
• One tbsp dried oregano
• Four garlic cloves, minced
• One tbsp red pepper flakes
• One pinch salt
• One cup mozzarella cheese, diced

Instructions

1. Set grill temperature to 350°F, then keep the lid closed for fifteen mins.
2. Slice the bread loaf in half lengthwise.
3. In a small bowl combine the mayonnaise, butter, garlic, salt, pepper flakes & oregano. Mix thoroughly.
4. Spread the butter mixture on the loaf halves & top it with parmesan & mozzarella cheese.
5. Put the bread on the grill grate. Grill for around 20 mins. Serve hot.

5. Tennessee Bacon

Preparation time: 10 mins

Cooking time: 20 mins

Servings: 4

Ingredients

- One lb smoked bacon, sliced
- One cup Tennessee or Bourbon Whiskey
- One cup apple juice
- One tbsp chicken rub
- Half cup white flour
- Half cup brown sugar
- One tsp ground black pepper

Instructions

1. Put the bacon slices into a big resealable bag.
2. Pour in a bowl the whisky and apple juice; add the chicken rub and whisk thoroughly. Add the seasoned liquid to the bacon and seal the bag.
3. Let the bacon marinate in the fridge for around half an hour.
4. In another resealable bag, add the brown sugar, black pepper & flour; shake well to mix.
5. Drain the bacon slices from the marinade & put them in the flour mixture bag; shake well to coat evenly. Then proceed with the net bacon slice.
6. Arrange the bacon slices on a baking pan in a single layer.
7. Set grill temperature to 350°F, then keep the lid closed for fifteen mins.
8. Bake the bacon slices until golden brown & crisp, around 20 mins. Serve.

6. Spicy Jalapeño Balls

Preparation time: 15 mins

Cooking time: 45 mins

Servings: 8

Ingredients

- Four oz cream cheese
- Half cup cheddar cheese, shredded
- One tbsp coriander, minced
- Six Jalapeño peppers
- Two lbs ground pork
- Two tbsp chicken rub

Instructions

1. Set grill temperature to 350°F, then keep the lid closed for fifteen mins.
2. Combine cheddar, coriander & cream cheese in a bowl and mix thoroughly.
3. Divide in half lengthwise and seed the peppers; spoon the cheese mix in each half. Divide again in half each stuffed half pepper.
4. Take a small handful of ground meat, flatten it, put a piece of pepper on it and wrap the meat around to make a meatball; shape it well in your hands. Repeat for each piece.
5. Season each meatball with the pork rub.
6. On the grill grate, put the balls straight & cook for around thirty mins, till browned & cooked through, flipping them at least once. Serve.

7. Bison & Wild Boar Sausage

Preparation time: 10 mins

Cooking time: 4 hours

Servings: 4

Ingredients

- Half pound Ground Wild Boar
- Half pound Ground Wild Bison
- One tsp Kosher Salt
- Half tsp sugar
- One tsp pork rub
- One tbsp yellow mustard
- Half tsp black pepper
- Half tsp onion powder

Instructions

1. In a bowl, combine all ingredients, being careful not to overmix. Cover with cling film and refrigerate for the night.
2. Shape the meat into a loaf, roll it in a cling film sheet and twist the ends to give it a regular shape. Unwrap slowly
3. Set grill temperature to 350°F, then keep the lid closed for fifteen mins.
4. Place the loaf directly onto the grill grate & cook for around three to four hours. When cooked, let the loaf cool for one hour at room temp.
5. Slice & serve.

8. Cajun Stuffed Peppers

Preparation time: 15 mins

Cooking time: 40 mins

Servings: 6

Ingredients

- Six large red bell peppers
- One pound ground pork
- One onion, chopped
- Two garlic cloves, chopped
- Two tbsp pork rub
- Half cup tomato sauce
- Two cups cooked rice
- One cup cooked black beans, drained
- One cup fresh corn
- Half cup cheddar cheese, grated

Instructions

1. Wash and dry the peppers; slice them in half and remove the seeds.
2. To prepare the stuffing, in a big frying pan, brown the ground pork, breaking any lump with a wooden spatula.
3. When browned, add garlic & onion and stir fry for three more mins. Add the tomato sauce, pork rub, black beans, corn & rice; cook till the flavors are mixed, around five mins. Let it cool.
4. Fill every pepper half with the prepared stuffing, taking care not to overmix.
5. Set the grill temp to 350°F, then keep the lid closed for 15 mins.
6. Arrange the peppers, filling side up, directly on the hot grill grate. Cook for around 35 mins.
7. When cooked, sprinkle the grated cheese on the peppers; close the grill lid and cook for five more mins, to melt the cheese. Serve.

9. Paprika Grilled Chicken with Hot Salsa

Preparation time: 10 mins

Cooking time: 45 mins

Servings: 6

Ingredients

For the chicken

- Six whole chicken legs
- Two tbsp olive oil
- One tbsp smoked paprika
- One tsp ground coriander
- One tsp ground turmeric
- Zest of one lime
- Half tsp kosher salt
- One tsp ground black pepper

For the salsa

- Four jalapeño peppers
- Four garlic cloves, chopped
- Six sprigs fresh coriander
- Two spring onions, chopped
- One tbsp lime juice
- Two tbsp maple syrup
- Half cup white wine vinegar
- One tsp kosher salt

Instructions

1. In a big bowl combine the chicken, smoked paprika, olive oil, lime zest, coriander, pepper & salt, mixing well to season. Cover it with cling film & put it in the refrigerator for 4 hours or overnight.
2. Set the grill temp to 350°F, then keep the lid closed for 15 mins.
3. Put the chicken thighs directly on the hot on the grill grates, skin side down.

4. Cook until perfectly grilled, around 40-45 mins.
5. In the meanwhile, prepare the hot salsa. Put the peppers on the hot grill grates, beside the chicken & cook for around 25-30 mins. Remove the peppers from the grill, let them cool a bit and remove seeds and stems Blend in a mixer the jalapeños with all the other salsa ingredient, pulsing until smooth.
6. Serve the chicken with the spicy jalapeño salsa.

10. Bacon Cheddar Baby Potatoes

Preparation time: 30 mins

Cooking time: 40 mins

Servings: 6

Ingredients

- Two lbs baby potatoes
- One quarter cup olive oil
- One tsp garlic powder
- One tsp onion powder
- One tbsp smoked paprika
- One tbsp dried chives
- Two cups cheddar cheese, shredded
- One lb cooked bacon, crumbled
- One bunch spring onions, chopped
- 4 tbsp sour cream

Instructions

1. Boil/microwave the baby potatoes till fork tender, then let them cool at room temp.
2. Mix the garlic powder, olive oil, paprika, chives & onion powder in a large bowl. Pour in the potatoes & toss to coat well in the seasoning. Place the potatoes on a paper-lined cookie tray; with a fork, lightly smash every potato to flatten.
3. Set the grill temp to 450°F, then keep the lid closed for 15 mins.
4. Grill the potatoes for around twenty to thirty mins till their color changes to golden & crispy, flipping them once. When cooked, sprinkle the potatoes with the bacon, spring onions & cheddar. Close the lid & grill for ten mins more to let the cheese melt.
5. Take the potatoes from the grill & season with the sour cream. Serve.

11. Skillet Spicy Nachos Dip

Preparation time: 15 mins

Cooking time: 50 mins

Servings: 10

Ingredients

- Two tbsp olive oil
- One red onion, diced
- One and half tsp kosher salt
- Two lbs ground beef
- Two tbsp beef rub
- Two cups roasted tomatoes with their juices
- Two cups cooked black beans, drained
- Half cup green chiles, diced
- One bunch spring onions, chopped
- Half cup white rice, uncooked

Instructions

1. Set the grill temp to 400°F, place a 12-inch cast-iron skillet on the grill, then keep the lid closed for 15 mins to preheat.
2. Once the grill temp is set, put the onions, oil & half tsp salt into the skillet. Close the lid & cook, stirring once or twice, till the onions are tender, around ten mins.
3. Add the meat and one tsp salt 1 tsp, then cook for about 15-20 mins till browned, breaking any lump with a wooden spatula. Add the beef rub and mix.
4. Add the beans, tomatoes, green chiles, rice, & one cup of water. Mix well to ensure the liquid is covering the rice.
5. Cover the skillet with a lid, close the grill lid & cook for

6. twenty to twenty-five mins or till the rice is completely cooked and all the liquid has been absorbed.
7. Remove the skillet lid & sprinkle the cheese on top; close the grill lid again, till the cheese melts.
8. Remove the dip from the grill, sprinkle with the green onions and serve with corn chips.

12. Red Onion Jam, Duck Confit & Goat Cheese Crostini

Preparation time: 5 mins

Cooking time: 45 mins

Servings: 6

Ingredients

- Two tbsp butter
- Three red onions, sliced
- Two garlic cloves, shopped
- 4 tbsp sugar
- Pepper
- 4 tbsp dry red wine
- One tbsp apple cider vinegar
- Zest of one lemon
- Four prepared confit duck legs
- One baguette, sliced
- Half cup herbed goat cheese, crushed
- Olive oil
- 4 tbsp pomegranate arils
- Sea salt
- Black pepper, crushed

Instructions

1. Set the grill temp to 350°F, then keep the lid closed for 15 mins.

2. In a pan over low heat melt the butter; add the garlic, onions & sugar, then season with sea salt. Cover & cook till softened & caramelized, around 20-30 mins. Take it from the heat & whisk in the vinegar, lemon zest & red wine. Set aside.

3. Line a cookie tray with bakery paper. Place the duck legs on the tray, skin side, & put the tray on the grill grate.Cook for around eight to ten mins, till the skin begins to crisp & the meat breaks easily with the fork. Remove from the grill and chop the meat with two forks.

4. In the meantime, drizzle every baguette slice with olive oil & season with salt & pepper. Put the slices on the hot grill grate & cook till the grill marks develop, & the bread gets golden.

5. Build the crostini putting on the grilled bread slices the red onion jam, pulled duck, goat cheese & pomegranate. Serve.

13. Grilled Teff Flatbread with Cilantro Sauce

Preparation time: 5 mins

Cooking time: 10 mins

Servings: 4

Ingredients

Flatbread

- Half cup teff flour
- One and three quarters cups water
- Half tsp salt
- One egg
- Olive oil

Cilantro Sauce

- Four garlic cloves, chopped
- Two bunches fresh coriander, chopped
- Two Jalapeño peppers, seeded & chopped
- One tsp kosher salt
- One tsp ground cardamom
- One tsp ground cumin
- Half tsp red pepper Flakes
- Three quarters cup olive oil
- Three quarters cup lemon juice

Instructions

1. Combine the 1-3/4 cups water & teff flour in a glass bowl. Cover Loosely & let it rise overnight in a warm place.
2. Set the grill temp to 350°F, place a cast-iron pan on the grill, then keep the lid closed for 15 mins to preheat.
3. Whisk the egg into the fermented tuff & season with the salt. Lightly oil the cast iron pan. Once the oil is hot, add a small amount of batter to the skillet, instantly turning the pan around to coat.
4. Cook till the bread has firmed. Repeat with the rest of the batter.Prepare the sauce: blend all the ingredients in a food processor till smooth. Serve with the hot bread.

34

14. Mandarin Wings

Preparation time: 5 mins

Cooking time: 30 mins

Servings: 2

Ingredients

- One bottle mandarin orange sauce
- Two tbsp chicken rub
- Two lbs chicken wings, drumettes separated

Instructions

1. In a bowl, coat the chicken wings in the mandarin sauce. Sprinkle the chicken rub onto the wings, mix well and marinate for 30 mins.
2. Set the grill temp to 350°F, then keep the lid closed for 15 mins.
3. Put the marinated wings straight on the hot grill grates & cook for thirty mins. Serve.

15. Bacon Wrapped Chicken Wing

Preparation time: 30 mins

Cooking time: 1 hour

Servings: 6

Ingredients

- Two lbs chicken wings
- Three cups beer
- Two tsp red pepper flakes
- One lb bacon strips
- Two tbsp chicken rub

Instructions

1. Cut the tips from the wings & throw them away.
2. Put the wings and red pepper flakes in a large bowl & cover with the beer. Refrigerate overnight.
3. Remove the wings from the brine & pat dry. Top generously with chicken rub.
4. Wrap each wing with a bacon strip.
5. Set the grill temp to 450°F, then keep the lid closed for 15 mins.
6. Put the wings straight on the hot grill grate, close the lid & cook for around thirty mins. Turn the wings & cook for thirty mins more or till the bacon becomes crispy & the chicken is completely cooked. Serve.

16. Grilled Shrimp Cocktail

Preparation time: 5 mins

Cooking time: 10 mins

Servings: 2

Ingredients

Main

- Two lbs shrimp
- Two tbsp olive oil
- One tsp Old Bay seasoning
- Italian Parsley, minced

Cocktail Sauce

- Half cup ketchup
- Two tbsp prepared horseradish
- Two tbsp lemon juice
- Ground black pepper
- Kosher salt

Instructions

1. Set the grill temp to 350°F, then keep the lid closed for 15 mins.
2. Shell and devein the shrimps, leaving the tails on. Mix the shrimp with oil & Old Bay seasoning in a large bowl. Put the shrimp on a cookie sheet.
3. Put the cookie sheet on the grill grate & cook till opaque, around five to seven mins.
4. Prepare the cocktail sauce: combine horseradish, lemon juice & ketchup. Season with pepper & salt.
5. In a bowl, pour the cocktail sauce on the grilled shrimp. Season the shrimps with minced parsley. Serve.

17. Grilled Shrimp Brochette

Preparation time: 20 mins

Cooking time: 20 mins

Servings: 6

Ingredients

- One lb large shrimps, shelled & deveined
- Six jalapeño peppers
- Eight oz Monterey Jack Cheese
- One lb bacon
- Two tbsp all-purpose rub

Instructions

1. Fillet the shrimps, slightly flatten & set aside. Core & seed the jalapeños & slice them into tiny slivers. Cut the cheese in pieces the same size as the peppers. Cut in half the bacon slices.
2. Put one jalapeño slice & one cheese slice inside each shrimp. Wrap every stuffed shrimp in the half bacon piece.
3. Season the shrimps with the all-purpose rub.
4. Set the grill temp to 400°F, then keep the lid closed for 15 mins.
5. Put the shrimps straight on the slightly oiled grill grate. Cook for around twenty mins, flipping once, till the shrimps change color & the bacon gets crisp.
6. Take the shrimps from the grill & let rest for 10 mins. Serve.

18. Roasted Garlic Herb Potatoes

Preparation time: 30 mins

Cooking time: 45 mins

Servings: 4

Ingredients

- Four large potatoes
- One tsp salt
- Two tbsp olive oil
- One tsp rosemary, minced
- One tsp thyme, minced
- Two garlic cloves, minced
- Two tsp flake salt
- One tsp chopped parsley

Instructions

1. Set the grill temp to 400°F, then keep the lid closed for 15 mins.
2. Cut potatoes into wedges & place them into cold water with 1 tsp salt for half an hour.
3. Mix the rosemary, oil, garlic & thyme in a big bowl. Take the potatoes from the frost water & dry them completely.
4. Toss the potatoes in the oil mixture & put them on a parchment-lined cookie sheet, in a single layer layer. Season with flake salt.
5. Put the cookie sheets on the grill grate & roast for thirty mins; turn the potatoes and cook for fifteen more minutes until golden & crispy.
6. Take the potatoes from the grill, sprinkle with parsley and serve with your favorite dipping sauce.

19. Grilled Prosciutto Asparagus

Preparation time: 20 mins

Cooking time: 15 mins

Servings: 6

Ingredients

- Two bunches asparagus
- Salt & Pepper
- Four oz prosciutto
- Olive oil
- Zest of one lemon
- Two tbsp balsamic vinegar, divided
- Three tbsp toasted pine nuts

Instructions

1. Set the grill temp to 400°F, then keep the lid closed for 15 mins.
2. Wash the asparagus & pat dry. Cut the bottom thirds of the stalks and throw them away.
3. Wrap a prosciutto slice around four to five stalks & put them on a parchment-lined cookie sheet. Sprinkle the asparagus with salt, olive oil, lemon zest & pepper.
4. Put the cookie sheet on the grill grate and close the lid. After five mins, flip the asparagus & drizzle with one tbsp of the balsamic vinegar.
5. Close the lid again & cook till the prosciutto becomes crispy & the asparagus is completely cooked, around five to eight mins.
6. Sprinkle the asparagus with pine nuts & drizzle with the leftover balsamic vinegar. Serve.

20. Smoked Guacamole

Preparation time: 25 mins

Cooking time: 30 mins

Servings: 6

Ingredients

- Seven cored & peeled avocados, halved
- One whole poblano chile
- Four ears corns, husked
- One quarter cup cilantro, chopped
- One quarter cup tomato, chopped
- One quarter cup red onion, chopped
- Two tbsp lime juice
- One tsp ground cumin
- One tbsp garlic, minced
- Chile powder to taste
- Pepper & salt

Instructions

1. Set the grill temp to 180°F, then keep the lid closed for 15 mins.
2. Put the avocados halves cut side up & smoke for ten mins.
3. Take the avocados from the grill & increase the temp to 450°F.
4. Put the corn & poblano pepper straight on the grill grate. Cook for fifteen to twenty mins until charred.
5. Take the corn from the cobs & set aside.
6. Put the hot poblano pepper in a small bowl, cover with cling film & wait for ten mins; the skin should peel off easily. Chop the pepper & add it to the corn kernels.
7. Mash the smoked avocados in a large mixing bowl, leaving some chunks. Add the corn, peppers & all leftover ingredients. Mix and season with salt & pepper. Serve.

21. Grilled Sweet Potatoes

Preparation time: 5 mins

Cooking time: 20 mins

Servings: 6

Ingredients

- Five large sweet potatoes
- One tbsp olive oil
- One tsp salt
- One tsp ground black pepper
- Half tsp onion powder

Instructions

1. Clean the sweet potatoes, peel them and cut into eighths lengthwise.
2. Put the slices in a bowl and season with salt, oil, onion powder & pepper, mixing thoroughly.
3. Set the grill temp to 480°F, then keep the lid closed for 15 mins.
4. Put the sweet potatoes wedges directly on the hot grill grate, cook for 35-40 minutes and serve.

22. Smoked Artichoke Dip

Preparation time: 15 mins

Cooking time: 1 hour

Servings: 8

Ingredients

- Ten garlic cloves
- Half cup parmesan cheese
- Olive oil
- Half cup cheddar cheese
- Half cup fontina cheese
- Half cup provolone cheese
- Half cup cream cheese
- Half cup mayonnaise
- One can artichokes
- Kosher salt
- Ground black pepper

Instructions

1. Set the grill temp to 350°F, then keep the lid closed for 15 mins.
2. In a small oven-safe pan, put garlic cloves & add sufficient olive oil to cover the garlic. Move it on grill & cook for around 35 to 40 mins. Garlic will be done when soft enough to smash with a fork. Take it from the grill & allow it to cool.
3. Drain the garlic and reserve the oil for another recipe. Put the garlic in a bowl & smash with the fork till it becomes a paste.
4. Combine the cheddar, parmesan, fontina & provolone cheeses. Reserve half cup of the mixture.
5. Mix the cheese mixture with the mayonnaise, cream cheese, artichokes & garlic. Season with salt & pepper & mix thoroughly.
6. Put the mixture in an oven-safe dish & sprinkle with the reserved half cup of cheese mixture. Put the dish on the grill grate and cook for around 60 mins.
7. Serve the dip with crackers or a sliced baguette.

23. Honey & Sage Skillet Cornbread

Preparation time: 10 mins

Cooking time: 25 mins

Servings: 6

Ingredients

- One cup all-purpose flour
- One cup + three tbsp yellow cornmeal
- One tbsp baking powder
- Half tsp baking soda
- Two tbsp granulated sugar
- Half tsp kosher salt
- Two tbsp fresh sage, minced
- One large egg, beaten
- One cup milk
- One can cream corn
- Half cup softened unsalted butter
- Butter, flaky salt & honey for serving

Instructions

1. Set the grill temp to 400°F, then keep the lid closed for 15 mins.
2. Put one cup cornmeal, the flour, baking soda, baking powder, salt, minced sage & sugar. Mix well.
3. In another bowl put the egg, creamed corn & milk. Stir well but don't beat too much.
4. Fold the dry ingredients into the wet ones.
5. Melt the butter in a cast iron skillet; sprinkle the skillet with the three reserved cornmeal tbsp. Pour the batter into the skillet & level it with a spatula.
6. Put the skillet on the grill grate, close the lid and cook for around 25 minutes.
7. Take it from the grill, let it rest for ten mins and cut into wedges. Serve hot with honey, flaky salt & butter.

24. Spicy Fries with Smoky Ketchup

Preparation time: 10 mins

Cooking time: 15 mins

Servings: 4

Ingredients

Chipotle Ketchup

- Two cans chipotle peppers in adobo sauce
- One tbsp olive oil
- One tsp onion powder
- One tsp garlic powder
- One cup tomato ketchup
- One tbsp sugar
- One tbsp cumin
- One tbsp chili powder
- Juice from one lime

Main

- Six potatoes
- Two tbsp butter, melted
- One tbsp beef rub
- 4 tbsp fresh parsley, chopped

Instructions

1. Finely chop the chipotle peppers & put them in a bowl along with all the other smoky ketchup ingredients. Mix well and let ret rest in the fridge one hour to let the flavors blend.
2. Set the grill temp to 440°F, then keep the lid closed for 15 mins.
3. Cut the potatoes into thick strips; put them in a bowl along with the beef rub & melted butter. Toss thoroughly to coat well.
4. Put the potato wedges on a parchment-lined cookie sheet & cook in the grill for around 10-15 mins. Take the potatoes from the grill, sprinkle with parsley and serve it with the smoky ketchup.

25. Smoked Nuts Mix

Preparation time: 5 mins

Cooking time: 1 hour

Servings: 4

Ingredients

- Two tbsp butter, melted
- One tsp sesame oil
- Two cup mixed nuts
- Half tsp chipotle hot sauce
- Half tsp Worcestershire sauce
- One tsp salt

Instructions

1. In a bowl combine all the ingredients excluding salt. Spread the mix onto a parchment-lined cookie sheet, in a single layer.
2. Set the grill temp to 260°F, then keep the lid closed for 15 mins.
3. Smoke the nuts for around one hour, stirring every fifteen mins. When done, remove the nuts and sprinkle with salt.
4. Let cool and serve or store in an air-tight container for as long as two weeks.

26. Smoked Chex Mix

Preparation time: 15 mins

Cooking time: 1 hour

Servings: 8

Ingredients

- Six tbsp butter
- Two tbsp soy sauce
- Half tbsp sea salt
- One tsp garlic powder
- Half tsp onion powder
- Three cups corn Chex cereals
- Three cups rice Chex cereals
- Three cups wheat Chex cereals
- One cup mixed nuts
- One cup bite-sized pretzels
- One cup minced Garlic

Instructions

1. Set the grill temp to 260°F, then keep the lid closed for 15 mins.
2. Melt the butter in a big oven-safe skillet. Add the soy sauce & seasonings, then all the remaining ingredients. Mix well to coat the nuts and cereals.
3. Put the skillet on the grate grill, close the lid & smoke for around one hour, stirring every fifteen mins.
4. Take the skillet out of the grill, let cool and serve. You can store the mix in an air-tight jar for up to two weeks.

27. Blue Cheese & Turkey Dip

Preparation time: 10 mins

Cooking time: 30 mins

Servings: 6

Ingredients

- Eight oz softened cream Cheese
- Half cup sour cream
- Half cup mayonnaise
- Two tbsp chicken rub
- One tsp sea salt
- Half cup hot sauce
- Two cup shredded cooked turkey
- One cup chopped mozzarella cheese
- One cup chopped cheddar cheese
- Half cup chopped blue cheese
- Four strips cooked bacon, crumbled

Instructions

1. Set the grill temp to 260°F, then keep the lid closed for 15 mins.
2. Mix the sour cream, cream cheese, rub, mayonnaise, salt & hot sauce in a food processor. Pulse till smooth.
3. Fold in the mozzarella, shredded turkey, bacon, blue cheese & cheddar. Transfer the mix to an ovenproof dish or skillet
4. Put the dish on the grill grate, close the lid & cook for around twenty to thirty mins, till the top color changes to golden brown & the dip start bubbling.
5. Serve with crackers, chips, crostini.

28. Ultimate Mexican Nachos

Preparation time: 15 mins

Cooking time: 25 mins

Servings: 4

Ingredients

- One bag tortilla chips
- Half cup fresh salsa
- One lb chorizo, sliced
- Two cups cooked turkey, shredded
- 4 tbsp chopped green onions
- 2 jalapeños peppers, sliced
- 4 tbsp green olives, pitted & chopped
- Half cup cheddar cheese, shredded
- Half cup sour cream
- Half cup prepared guacamole sauce
- 4 tbsp fresh cilantro, chopped

Instructions

1. Set the grill temp to 260°F, then keep the lid closed for 15 mins.
2. Spread out evenly the tortilla chips on a big cookie sheet. Sprinkle on the chips the salsa, chicken, & chorizo. Season the nachos with the jalapeños, green onions, cheese & olives.
3. Put the cookie sheet on the grill grate, close the lid & cook for around ten to fifteen mins, till the cheese melts & the nachos are completely heated.
4. Take the nachos out of the grill and serve with the guacamole, cilantro & sour cream.

29. Onion Dip

Preparation time: 30 mins

Cooking time: 45 mins

Servings: 8

Ingredients

- One tbsp butter
- One tbsp vegetable oil
- Two sweet onions, chopped
- Half tsp sugar
- One tsp salt
- Half tsp garlic powder
- One tsp ground black pepper
- Half tsp dried thyme
- Half cup beef stock
- One tbsp soy sauce
- One tbsp bourbon whisky
- Half cup sour cream
- Eight oz cream cheese
- Two tbsp chives, chopped

Instructions

1. Set the grill temp to 480°F, then keep the lid closed for 15 mins.
2. Place the butter & the vegetable oil in a disposable foil skillet directly on the hot grill grate. Once butter is melted, take the skillet from the grill & whisk in the sugar, diced onions, pepper, thyme, garlic powder & salt.
3. Add the Worcestershire sauce, bourbon, & beef stock; mix well.
4. Put the skillet back on the grill grate, close the lid and cook until the onions stirring occasionally, until they become soft & color changes to golden brown. Take the skillet from the grill & allow the onions to cool completely.
5. In the meanwhile, mix the cream cheese & sour cream in a big bowl, until the mix is smooth.
6. Add the cold onions & chopped chives, mixing until combined; season with salt & pepper.
7. Cover with cling film & cool in the fridge. Serve.

30. Smoked Trout

Preparation time: 10 mins

Cooking time: 2 hours

Servings: 6

Ingredients

- Eight trout fillets
- One gallon water
- 4 tbsp kosher salt
- Half cup brown sugar
- One tbsp black pepper
- Two tbsp soy sauce

Instructions

1. Prepare the brine: in a big bowl mix the water, soy sauce, brown sugar, pepper & salt, then whisk till sugar & salt are dissolved.
2. Add the trout fillets to the brine, cover with cling film an let marinate for one hour or more in the fridge.
3. Set the grill temp to 250°F, then keep the lid closed for 15 mins.
4. Take the fish fillets from the brine & pat dry. Put the fillets directly on the grill grate, close the lid and cook for around two hours. When the fillets turn opaque & begins to flake take them from the grill & serve.

31. Southern Chicken Wings

Preparation time: 15 mins

Cooking time: 30 mins

Servings: 4

Ingredients

- Two lbs chicken wings
- Two tsp kosher salt
- One tbsp Cajun rub
- One tbsp chicken rub
- One tbsp pork rub

Instructions

1. In a bowl, coat the wings in the Cajun, chicken & pork rub. Sesaon with salt and mix well.
2. Set the grill temp to 350°F, then keep the lid closed for 15 mins.
3. Place the seasoned wings directly on the hot grill grate & cook for around thirty mins or till the skin becomes brown & the meat is juicy. Serve

32. Baked Potatoes with Cheese & Pulled Pork

Preparation time: 15 mins

Cooking time: 1 hour

Servings: 6

Ingredients

- Four potatoes
- 2 tbsp olive oil
- 2 tsp sea salt
- Two tbsp melted butter
- Three cups pulled pork
- Four tbsp BBQ sauce
- One cup mozzarella cheese, chopped
- One cup cheddar cheese, grated
- One green onion, minced
- Four tbsp sour cream
- Four slices cooked bacon, crumbled

Instructions

1. Set the grill temp to 450°F, then keep the lid closed for 15 mins.
2. Rub the potatoes with olive oil & season with salt evenly. Place the potatoes directly on the hot grill grate & cook for around 45 mins.
3. Take the potatoes from the grill, cut them in half and scoop out about 70% of the potato, leaving 1/4 inch on the skin. Brush the inside with melted butter, put them on a cookie sheet & back into the grill. Cook for around five mins.
4. Combine in a bowl the BBQ sauce, pulled pork, cheddar cheese & mozzarella.
5. Stuff the potato halves with the mix, close the grill lid & wait for the cheese to melt. Take the potatoes from the grill, top with crumbled bacon, sour cream & minced onions. Serve.

33. Deep Dish Pizza

Preparation time: 15 mins

Cooking time: 30 mins

Servings: 4

Ingredients

- Pizza dough for four
- One tbsp olive oil
- Half cup pizza sauce
- Two cups mozzarella cheese
- One tsp fresh oregano
- Parmesan cheese to taste
- One tsp fresh basil
- One lb Italian sausage, sliced
- Half green bell pepper, chopped
- Half red bell pepper, chopped
- Two tbsp onions, diced
- Fresh mushrooms to taste, sliced
- Black olives to taste, pitted
- Pepperoni to taste, sliced

Instructions

1. Set the grill temp to 450°F, then keep the lid closed for 15 mins.
2. Coat a twelve-inch cast-iron skillet with olive oil. Put the dough into the skillet pressing it on the bottom, moving to the sides.
3. Assemble the pizza: spread the pizza sauce on the dough top & add the red & green bell peppers, mushrooms, sausage, pepperoni, onions & olives. Last, sprinkle grated parmesan & mozzarella on the top & season with basil & oregano.
4. Put the skillet on the grill grate, close the lid & cook for around 25 to 30 mins.
5. When coked, let the pizza rest for five mins, slice it & serve.

34. Bacon Chicken Hot Skewers

Preparation time: 3 hours

Cooking time: 20 mins

Servings: 6

Ingredients

- Half cup ranch dressing
- Half tsp garlic powder
- Two tbsp chili Sauce
- Half tsp dried oregano
- One lb chicken breast, cubed
- One red onion, cubed
- One green bell pepper, cubed
- Eight strips bacon, sliced

Instructions

1. Combine the garlic powder, ranch dressing, chili sauce & oregano in a large bowl. Add the cubed chicken breast & toss to coat well. Cover with cling film & marinate in the fridge for up to 3 hours.
2. Set the grill temp to 450°F, then keep the lid closed for 15 mins.
3. Assemble the skewers: alternate the onion wedges, peppers, bacon slices, & chicken. Go alternating & complete off every skewer with an onion wedge & pepper cube.
4. Place the skewers directly on the hot grill grate. You can put a piece of foil under each skewer's end to make flipping them easier & to stop them from burning.
5. Grill for around five mins each side, turning a quarter each time, 20 mins total. Take the skewers from the grill & serve.

35. Bacon Onion Rings

Preparation time: 10 mins

Cooking time: 1 hour

Servings: 6

Ingredients

- Sixteen slices bacon
- Two sliced big onions
- One tbsp chili garlic sauce
- One tbsp yellow mustard
- One tsp honey

Instructions

1. Wrap every bacon piece around a single onion ring; go on till the bacon is finished.
2. To save bacon from unraveling throughout the cooking, pierce it with a skewer.
3. Set the grill temp to 450°F, then keep the lid closed for 15 mins.
4. In a bowl, combine yellow mustard, honey & chili garlic sauce mixing thoroughly.
5. Put the rings directly on the grill grate & cook for around 1hr 30 mins, turning after forty-five mins. Serve with the dipping sauce.

36. Indian Chicken Wings

Preparation time: 30 mins

Cooking time: 50 mins

Servings: 4

Ingredients

Main

- Quarter cup yogurt
- Two tbsp scallions, chopped
- One tbsp fresh coriander, chopped
- Two tsp fresh ginger, minced
- One tsp garam masala
- Half tsp salt
- One tsp ground black pepper
- Half pound chicken wings

Yogurt Sauce

- Quarter cup yogurt
- Two tbsp mayonnaise
- Two tbsp cucumber, diced
- Two tsp lemon juice
- Half tsp ground cumin
- Cayenne Pepper, to taste

Instructions

1. Mix scallions, yogurt, ginger, cilantro, salt, garam masala, & pepper in a blender & process till smooth. Pour the mix into a big bowl, add the chicken wings and mix to coat well. Cover the bowl with cling film and put it on the fridge for four to eight hours. Remove the wings from the marinade; throw the marinade away.
2. Set the grill temp to 360°F, then keep the lid closed for 15 mins.
3. Arrange the wings directly on the grill grate. Cook for around 45-50 mins, or till the skin color changes to brown & starts to crisp. Flip once/twice while cooking to avoid sticking.
4. In the meantime, mix all of the sauce ingredients in a bowl; refrigerate it till the wings are ready.
5. When the wings are completely cooked transfer to a platter & serve with the yogurt sauce.

37. Caramelized Bacon Bites

Preparation time: 10 mins

Cooking time: 25 mins

Servings: 2

Ingredients

- Half cup brown sugar
- One tbsp ground fennel
- Two tsp kosher salt
- One tsp ground black pepper
- One lb pork belly, diced

Instructions

1. Prepare an aluminum foil, around 12 x 36", fold it in half & crimp the borders to create a sort of rim on the edges. Poke some holes in the bottom to release come of the bacon's fat & make it crispier.
2. Set the grill temp to 350°F, then keep the lid closed for 15 mins.
3. Mix in a bowl the ground fennel, brown sugar, black pepper & salt.
4. Add the cubed pork belly into the mix & toss till well coated. Place the seasoned pork onto the aluminum foil.
5. Place the foil on the grill grates & cook till the pieces become crispy, bubbly & glazed, around 20 to 30 mins. Serve.

38. Hasselback Style Potatoes

Preparation time: 30 mins

Cooking time: 2 hours

Servings: 6

Ingredients

- Six large potatoes
- One lb bacon, sliced
- Half cup butter
- Black pepper
- Salt
- One cheddar cheese, shredded
- Three scallions, chopped

Instructions

1. Put two wooden spoons on the sides of a potato side to be sure not to cut them all the way. Cut into thin chips, taking care to leave potato leaving around one quarter inch attached to the bottom.
2. Cut the bacon slices in small squares and put them between the potato slices.
3. Put the potatoes on a large oven-safe skillet. Season the potatoes with salt & pepper & top with cold butter slices.
4. Set the grill temp to 350°F, then keep the lid closed for 15 mins.
5. Place the skillet on the grill grates, close the lid & cook for 2 hrs. Drizzle the potatoes with the melted butter around every thirty mins.
6. When the potatoes are ready, sprinkle them with cheddar & put them back into the grill to melt the cheese.
7. Take the potatoes from the grill, sprinkle with chopped scallions & serve.

39. Granny's Cornbread

Preparation time: 10 mins

Cooking time: 25 mins

Servings: 4

Ingredients

- One cup all-purpose flour
- One cup cornmeal
- One tbsp sugar
- Two tsp baking powder
- Half tsp salt
- Three tbsp Butter
- One cup milk
- One egg, lightly beaten

Instructions

1. Combine in a mixing bowl the cornmeal, flour, baking powder, salt & sugar.
2. In a saucepan melt the butter. Take it from the heat, & whisk in the egg & milk.
3. Combine milk-egg mixture with dry ingredients & whisk it, taking care not to overmix.
4. Grease a 9-inch square cooking pan, pour the batter in and level with a spatula.
5. Set the grill temp to 375°F, then keep the lid closed for 15 mins.
6. Cook the cornbread till it starts to detach from the pan sides & the top starts to brown nicely, around 25-35 mins.
7. Take the bread from the grill, let cool a little & serve with more cold butter.

40. Smoked Spicy Olives

Preparation time: 10 mins

Cooking time: 20 mins

Servings: 4

Ingredients

- One lb mixed olives
- One tbsp olive oil
- Zest of one orange
- Zest of one lemon
- Half tbsp red pepper flakes
- Half tbsp dried fennel seeds
- Three dried bay leaves
- Four thyme sprigs
- Four rosemary sprigs

Instructions

1. Set the grill temp to 250°F, then keep the lid closed for 15 mins.
2. Place the olives in an oven-proof skillet & put them on the grill grate. Smoke at low temperature for around twenty to thirty mins.
3. When the olives are smoked to your taste, take them from the grill & let cool. When chilled, mix olive oil, smoked olives, lemon zest, orange zest, red pepper flakes, bay leaves, fennel, thyme & rosemary. Serve.

41. Spinach Mini Quiches

Preparation time: 15 mins

Cooking time: 15 mins

Servings: 8

Ingredients

- One tbsp olive oil
- Cooking spray
- Half yellow onion, diced
- Three cups spinach
- Ten eggs
- Four oz cheddar, shredded
- One quarter cup fresh basil
- One tsp kosher salt
- Half tsp black pepper

Instructions

1. Prepare a 12-serving muffin tin; grease generously with cooking spray
2. Heat the oil in a skillet, add the onions & cook on medium heat whisking regularly till softened, around 7 mins. Add the spinach & cook till wilted, around one minute further.
3. Let the combination cool, then mince it on a chopping board.
4. Set the grill temp to 350°F, then keep the lid closed for 15 mins.
5. Crack the eggs in a bowl and stir till frothy. Add the onions, spinach, cheese, spinach, basil, salt & pepper. Mix thoroughly to combine. Pour the egg mix into the muffin cups.
6. Put the muffin tin on the grill grate, close the lid & bake till the eggs color turn to brown, and the muffins have puffed up & are set, around 20 mins.
7. Take the tin out of the grill, let cool a bit, remove the muffins and serve.

42. Bloody Mary Wings

Preparation time: 20 mins

Cooking time: 1 hour

Servings: 6

Ingredients

- Two lbs chicken wings
- Two cups Bloody Mary mix
- Three tbsp celery salt

Instructions

1. Set the grill temp to 350°F, then keep the lid closed for 15 mins.
2. Season the wings with celery salt & place them directly on the grill grate. Cook for around thirty mins, regularly flipping till the wings become crispy & golden.
3. Remove the wings from the grill, place them into a disposable aluminum skillet, pour the Bloody Mary & mix to coat them well.
4. Cover the skillet with aluminum foil and place them back into the grill for a further thirty mins.
5. Remove the wings from the grill, arrange them on a serving dish and serve.

43. Beef Thai Satay

Preparation time: 10 mins

Cooking time: 10 mins

Servings: 6

Ingredients

- Two lbs flatiron steak
- One bottle carne asada marinade
- Two garlic cloves, minced
- Two scallions, chopped
- Four tbsp peanuts, chopped
- Peanut sauce as needed
- Two limes

Instructions

1. Cut the flatiron steak into half-inch strips with a sharp knife. Place the strips in a bowl, add the marinade, scallions & garlic. Mix well to combine. Cover with cling film and refrigerate for at least one hour or overnight.
2. Drain the meat from the marinade & thread every piece on a bamboo skewer.
3. Set the grill temp to 450°F, then keep the lid closed for 15 mins.
4. Grill your satays, flipping once, for three to four mins each side.
5. In the meantime, place the peanut sauce a bowl. Remove the skewers from the grill, arrange them on a serving dish, sprinkle with the chopped peanuts & serve the peanut sauce & lime wedges.

44. Honey Soy Chicken Skewers

Preparation time: 15 mins

Cooking time: 15 mins

Servings: 6

Ingredients

- Four chicken breasts, diced
- One tbsp olive oil
- Two tsp garlic, minced
- Two tsp Onion powder
- Three quarters cup rice vinegar
- Four tbsp soy sauce
- Three tbsp honey
- Juice from two limes
- Black pepper
- Salt

Instructions

1. Combine all the ingredients, including the chicken, in a large bowl; mix thoroughly to combine well.
2. Cover the bowl with cling film & refrigerate overnight.
3. Set the grill temp to 450°F, then keep the lid closed for 15 mins.
4. Thread the marinated chicken on twelve skewers and place them directly on the hot grill grate. Turn the skewers a couple of time ang grill until cooked, around 15 mins.
5. Remove the skewers and serve with vegetables of your choice.

45. Grilled Vegetables & Smoked Hummus

Preparation time: 15 mins

Cooking time: 40 mins

Servings: 4

Ingredients

- Half cup chickpeas, cooked
- One third cup tahini
- One tbsp garlic, minced
- Six tbsp olive oil
- One tsp salt
- Four tbsp lemon juice
- One red onion, sliced
- Two cups butternut squash
- Two cups brussels sprouts
- Two cups cauliflower, cut into florets
- Two Portobello mushrooms, sliced
- Black pepper
- Salt

Instructions

1. For the hummus, set the grill temp to 200°F, then keep the lid closed for 15 mins.
2. Rinse & drain the chickpeas, place them on a cookie sheet and place the sheet on grill grate. Smoke at low temperature for around twenty mins.
3. Remove the smoked chickpeas and combine in a food processor bowl with tahini, three tbsp olive oil, garlic, lemon juice & salt; process till combined well, taking care not to over process, for better texture. Place the hummus in a bowl and set aside.
4. For the vegetables, set the grill temp to 450°F, then keep the lid closed for 15 mins.

5. Place all the vegetables on a cookie sheet and drizzle them with 3 tbsp olive oil. Place the sheet on the grill grate & cook for around 20 mins till the vegetables brown nicely & are completely cooked.
6. Arrange the vegetables on a serving platter, season with salt & black pepper and serve with the hummus and warm pita bread.

46. Potatoes and Venison Pie

Preparation time: 10 mins

Cooking time: 40 mins

Servings: 4

Ingredients

- Two lbs ground venison
- Two tbsp olive oil
- Two cans peas
- Two cans mushroom soup
- Twenty-eight oz frozen potatoes tots
- Salt & pepper

Instructions

1. Heat the oil in an oven-safe skillet. Add the venison & stir fry until nicely browned. Drain the venison from the skillet, get rid of the excess fat & put the venison back into the skillet.
2. Add the peas and mushroom soup, season with salt & pepper & mix well. Arrange the tots on top of the mix.
3. Set the grill temp to 350°F, then keep the lid closed for 15 mins.
4. Place the skillet on the grill grates, close the lid & cook for around thirty mins. Serve it warm.

47. Sweet Potato & Adobo Mayonnaise

Preparation time: 15 mins

Cooking time: 30 mins

Servings: 4

Ingredients

- Four sweet potatoes
- Three tbsp olive oil
- One tbsp salt
- One tsp black pepper
- One cup mayonnaise
- Two chipotle peppers in adobo sauce
- Juice from two limes

Instructions

1. Set the grill temp to 350°F, then keep the lid closed for 15 mins.
2. Peel the potatoes & cut them into sticks. Toss them in a big bowl along with salt, pepper & olive oil.
3. Arrange the potatoes sticks on a cookie sheet, put the sheet on the grill grate, close the lid & cook for around 25 mins, stirring a couple times, till the fries become crispy & nicely browned.
4. In the meanwhile, mix chiles, lime juice & mayonnaise in a blender & process till smooth.
5. Remove the fries from the grill, arrange them on a serving platter & serve along with the adobo mayonnaise.

48. Grilled Corn Salsa

- Black Pepper
- Salt

Preparation time: 25 mins

Cooking time: 15 mins

Servings: 6

Ingredients

- Four corn husks
- Four ripe tomatoes, chopped
- Half cup cilantro, chopped
- One tsp garlic powder
- One tsp onion powder
- Two tbsp jalapeño peppers, chopped
- Juice from one lime

Instructions

1. Set the grill temp to 450°F, then keep the lid closed for 15 mins.
2. Put the corn directly on the hot grill grate & cook till it is completely charred; discard the husk & cut the kernels from the cob.
3. Mix the corn with all the remaining ingredients & refrigerate till ready to serve.

49. Smoked Shrimps & Scallops Ceviche

Preparation time: 20 mins

Cooking time: 1 hour

Servings: 4

Ingredients

- One lb scallops, shelled
- One lb shrimps, shelled & deveined
- One tbsp olive oil
- Juice & zest from one lime
- Juice from one lemon
- Juice from one orange
- One tsp garlic powder
- One tsp onion Powder
- Two tsp salt
- Half tsp black pepper
- One avocado, diced
- Half red onion, diced
- One Tbsp cilantro, chopped
- Half tsp red pepper flakes

Instructions

1. Combine the scallops, shrimp & olive oil in an oven-proof dish & mix well to coat.
2. Set the grill temp to 200°F, then keep the lid closed for 15 mins.
3. Place the dish on the grill grates & smoke the seafood for forty-five mins.
4. In the meanwhile, mix in a big bowl all the other ingredients, stirring thoroughly to combine the flavors.
5. Allow the shrimp & scallops to cool, cut them in half & add them in the bowl along with all the other ingredients.
6. Cover the bowl with cling film & put the ceviche in to fridge for two to three hours to allow the flavors to mix. Serve with corn chips.

50. Prosciutto Shrimps with Apricot Salsa

Preparation time: 20 mins

Cooking time: 12 mins

Servings: 4

Ingredients

- Two lb shrimps, shelled & deveined
- Eight slices Italian prosciutto ham
- Four Apricots, diced
- Two tbsp balsamic vinegar
- Two tbsp honey
- One jalapeño pepper, chopped
- Two tbsp fresh basil, chopped
- Black pepper
- Salt

Instructions

Cut the prosciutto slices in strips, lengthwise; spiral wrap the prosciutto strips around every shrimp and secure with a wooden skewer.

For the apricot salsa: combine in a mixing bowl the vinegar, apricots, jalapeño, honey, basil, salt.

Set the grill temp to 450°F, then keep the lid closed for 15 mins.

Place the prosciutto-covered shrimps on the grill grate & cook for around 5 mins on each side.

Take the shrimps from the grill & serve along with the apricot salsa.

Lightning Source UK Ltd.
Milton Keynes UK
UKHW020816180621
385734UK00005B/27